What

Candy has a wonderful habit of taking you from what you thought was obvious and putting a whole new twist into your understanding! Internationally known for the way she delivers energetic and engaging presentations, Candy delivers the same exciting approach in this book. Don't dance around the issues any more, let this book teach you how to get in rhythm with those you work with.
-Steven Iwersen, Founder of Aurora Pointe LLC

Candy Whirley has put together a brilliant exploration of behavioral styles that will make you think, laugh….and *recognize* yourself and others! The discoveries and insights from this book will help you have greater influence with people in all areas of your life.
-Cathy Newton, author of *Living in Full Swing*

i

This book turns frustration into fascination! She delivers bright insights into behavior that will change your mind, change your outlook and make you laugh until you hurt!
 -Tyler Henderson, IBM WebSphere Senior Software Specialist

Candy Whirley is an exciting presenter and I love the upbeat and helpful message she describes so well in this fun and interesting book.
-Chuc Barnes, MinutesCount!

FINALLY,
A GUIDEBOOK TO HELP
PEOPLE LIVE AND WORK
BETTER TOGETHER AND STOP
DRIVING EACH OTHER
CRAZY!

IT TAKES
4
TO TANGO!

CANDY WHIRLEY

CorPax Press
Kansas City, MO

It Takes 4 To Tango

ISBN: 0-9823988-0-8

Library of Congress Control Number:
2009902537

Edited by Karen L. Anderson, president of
ACTS-ion Solutions, LLC

First Printing April 2009
Second Printing October 2014

For information contact the author:
Candy Whirley
SBG Services, LLC
cwhirley@kc.rr.com
www.candywhirley.com

CorPax Press
Kansas City, MO

Table of Contents

About the Author

 From the Hawaiian Islands to London, England, to Seoul Korea Candy Whirley is famous for her high energy enthusiasm, innovative training activities, and contagious sense of humor. She is a dynamic speaker dedicated to sharing over 25 years of her professional expertise to help professionals improve their job performance and achieve their personal goals. In Candy's words, ***"Get along, to get it done and make it FUN!"***

She brings a wealth of experience from many industries including: training, retail, customer service (certified by International Customer Service Association - ICSA), restaurant, entertainment, management, and youth ministry. Candy is a past President and currently serves on the Board of the Kansas City Chapter of the National Speakers Association.

You may recognize Candy, she is a former Kansas City Chiefs Chiefette, performed at Starlight Theater in Kansas City, and modeled for the Kansas City Star Magazine.

Her desire to speak better and have better relationships compelled Candy to major in Speech Communications with an emphasis on Human Relations for her Bachelor of Science degree. She graduated Cum Laude! Later she continued her education to include a Masters of Management degree.

In 2001 SBG Services, LLC was born. SBG stands for *Sent by God*. Candy truly believes her journey on earth is to teach people about themselves and how to get along better. She wants peace on Earth, one audience at a time!

Since the start of her business, she has spoken nationally and internationally to over 100,000 people from over 500 different companies. Her participants have come to know how to work and live successfully and harmoniously with people who are not like them.

Candy lives in Kansas City with her husband, Brad, and their two dogs Bubba and Tessa. She has two grown children, Jordan and Alex. Her greatest joy is becoming the sassiest "Grammy" in the Midwest for her three grandsons, Corban, Paxton and Hudson.

Note to the Reader

In the dance world, it takes two humans to tango, but in the real world, you will meet lots of people with "animal" personalities with their own ways of dancing. With them, ***It Takes 4 To Tango!***

This book was written by request. I speak nationally and internationally, and I teach the Animal Game almost everywhere I go. When I return from my speaking trips, my inbox is full of requests and comments about the Animal Game. Much of the research for this book is from my participants, so you just might see something you said during your Animal Game experience. Thank you all for encouraging me to write this book. Enjoy!

--Candy Whirley, 2009

Dedication
To Brad, my rock and analytical Owl.

Thanks
To my BSFs (Best Speaker Friends), Cathy, Steven, JoAnn and Marty. You all pushed me, helped me and laughed with me through this process. Thanks to Henrick who got me started on this journey.

Appreciation
To all my participants from all over the world for teaching me a thing or two about your "animals"!

Acknowledgement
Mom, Dad, Jordan, Alex, Lavi, Corban, Paxton, Hudson Ty, Doug, and Curt for my joy and laughter☺

Buckle up! Your adventure is about to begin.

INTRODUCTION

Recently, you may have experienced my **Animal Game** in person or by listening to my CD, and you want to share your experience with someone else or review what you learned.

In *It Takes 4 to Tango !,* I will describe the four "animals," or the four basic personality types with whom you most likely "dance" through work and life. For both clarification and amusement, "tango" symbolizes the metaphorical dances of the figurative animals. You will learn the strengths, weaknesses, irritations, and affirmations for each type. You will discover who drives you crazy and why.

"The Real Deal," "The Tango," "What I Know," "Tidbits," "Dark Side," "How to Overcome," and "Best Job" are sections that will clarify each personality type. In each section of this book I have laid out the questions and answers of my much requested **Animal Game.** You will read the questions and the answers I have received from my participants across the country. Also, in each animal chapter you will find "Candy's Corner" to find the sweet treat each animal craves and "Whirling Around" for flirting on the dance floor. (All puns and fun are intended.)

You may be familiar with Myers Briggs, DISC, SELF, or Real Colors personality profiles. The Animal Game is very similar to these personality indicators. As a matter of fact, I wrote many research papers in pursuit of my Masters in Management degree on all the personality indicators. The **Animal Game** is a simple, fun, and safe way for people to understand one another's personalities, quirks and tango moves.

What I have seen with organizations that I have worked with is people treat others as they themselves want to be treated instead of treating others as *those others* want to be treated. So what happens then? People have communication breakdown, negotiation let down, and delegation fall down! We can get along better and experience beautiful dances together if we simply learn the steps of one another's dances. Let's get started.

First, as you read about each personality of the animals, think only about yourself. Figure out who you are, which characteristics sound more like who you are at work and at home, and realize they may be different. You will also catch yourself feeling like you are a little of one animal and a little of another. Most people have a primary and a secondary personality style. Concentrate on the primary personality. I promise you, as you read further you will find who you truly are.

"It was amazing to see some employees who determined which "Animal" they were from the first portion of the training: some came to the realization quietly while others were more boisterous."

--Brandy W., Assistant Vice President, Workshop Participant

Next, after you have figured out who you are, start thinking about the people you work with: your peers, bosses, or clients. Analyze these people, but don't tell them! When you figure out first who you are, then who they are, that's when the magic happens. You learn how to dance *their* tango!

Last, make sure you do the same analysis with your family members--all of them! You will find your relationships changing once you understand the similarities and the differences. Which animal is Dad, which animal is Mom and Grandma? Then teach everyone in the family what you know. Make it a family game night--**The Animal Game!**

The latter chapters provide real-life insights and applications for learning the variations of tangoing with animals all around you. Communication scripts and tips will help you become an expert in relationship management.

I am sure you will have fun with the Animal Game information. I would love to hear your comments after reading and learning from **It Takes 4 to Tango!**

"I am going to play the Animal Game with my CSR's [customer service representatives]. I want them to see why they have such a hard time getting along. Plus, it will help me see if we have people in the correct positions. I want to sincerely thank you."

--J Martin, Supervisor
Workshop Participant

Please email me with questions and comments at
<u>cwhirley@kc.rr.com</u>

Chapter I

CHAMELEON People

The Real Deal

Chameleon in Greek: "Chamai" (on the ground, on the earth) and "leon" (lion): Earth Lion. Chameleons can rotate their eyes, focus separately and observe two separate objects at the same time. They are capable of extending their tongues out of their mouth at a rapid rate.
Wikipedia, 3/4/09.

Chameleon Tango

When you see a Chameleon dance, you will see the Y-M-C-A, the Cha Cha Slide, and most of all Free Style. Chameleons love their dance! Just ask them. They will change their dance steps to go with the crowd. If the crowd is on the tables doing the YMCA, so are they. If the crowd is low key at the wedding reception, the Chameleons will be low key. But they will be in front, trying to get the party started!

What I Know

Think about what happens when a real Chameleon gets on you or on a leaf. They change to match the environment. Chameleon people love change. In a professional environment, they must have a job that requires change in their day-to-day work, or they go crazy. Chameleons like to have many options when it comes to problem solving. I have been told at my workshops, "Chameleons talk too much." They love to talk, but listening is left up to the Lambs.

Animal Game Questions
The following answers come from
the Chameleons all over the
country.

**What are things Chameleons
are really good at?**

Risk taking
Creativity
Flexibility
Change management
Working with other people
Having fun

**What do the other animals
REALLY think about
Chameleons?**

Wishy-washy
Can't make a decision
Non-trustworthy
Flighty
Want change just for the sake of
change
Party people
Outlandish

3

What ONE animal of the other three animals "bugs" the Chameleons the most? Why?

The answer most given across the country from the Chameleons is the Owls. The Owls frustrate the Chameleons because they are the Chameleons' polar opposite. *See the chart on page 69.* Owls are very organized, everything is black and white, and there is only one way to do something--the right way. Chameleons believe the Owls can be too set in their way.

Note: This particular question has been answered in many different ways. Although the Owls are the most popular answer, the Chameleons sometimes choose other animals, too.

How do the other animals best communicate with the Chameleon for the best results?

Chameleons sincerely want to visit with you if you have an issue with them. No appointment is necessary, and they are open to many options for solutions. Chameleons like to be asked for their ideas for solutions or for handling issues in the workplace. By the way, Chameleons like you to approach them with enthusiasm and passion.

Tidbits to Remember

If you work with Chameleons, "Get Flexible."
They are people-oriented/leaders
Their motivation is FUN.

Dark Side (Sharp tongue)

Under pressure and stress, the Chameleons tend to say things they just wish they could reel back in. They are not the best at thinking things through before speaking. They say it, and then apologize. So if you see this side, there is usually something wrong at the Chameleon's work or home.

How to Overcome

To lighten up Chameleons' dark side, give them change and let them talk. Chameleons love to talk things out. They may be a little loud at first, but be patient and just listen.

Let me explain what I mean by change. They love change and when Chameleons don't have change in their lives they get antsy or bored, and they need something new or different. For their professional life, cross training is ideal. Put them in charge of the holiday committee. At home, let them re-decorate a lot. Let the Chameleons choose a few activities for the vacation.

Best Job

Chameleon people are very flexible. Any job that requires risk, persuasion, change and fun will work!

Speaker
Public Relations
Marketing
Sales
Politician
Server
Entrepreneur

Candy's Corner

How do Chameleons eat M&M's?
They cut a slight corner off the
package put it up to their mouth
and eat them all at once!

What is their favorite candy bar?
Almond Joy: sometimes you feel
like a nut!

Whirling Around

(For adults only!)
Chameleons flirt with everyone
and they flirt a lot. Why? Because
it is so easy for Chameleons. They
are social butterflies.

Chapter II

LION People

The Real Deal

These intimidating animals mark the area with urine, roar menacingly to warn intruders, and chase off animals that encroach on their turf. Lions have been celebrated throughout history for their courage and strength. nationalgeographic.com Sept. 2008

Lion Tango

When you see a Lion dance, you will most likely see them doing the Argentine Tango....why? Because they can be in charge! Lions throw their partners around and command their partners to stay in sync with the music, the steps and their leader.

What I Know

What do Lions like to do the most?
Be in charge! Lions are results
oriented, goal driven and
constantly searching for the
bottom-line. If you work or live
with Lions, you know they don't
like to have a drawn-out discussion
about any issue. They want the
Reader's Digest version of a story
or problem. Everyone working or
living with a Lion needs to know
you must get to the point fast.
Think bullet points at all times
when speaking to a Lion!

*"I had to fire a manager. She had
a Lion personality, so that made it
easier for me to come out and say
you've been terminated. After it
was over I felt pretty good about the
way that the whole thing went
down. Some of the things that I
learned in your workshop helped
me with this process. Thank you!!!"*
--Ruth S., Director
Workshop Participant

Animal Game Questions

Around the country, Lions
answered these questions.

What are things Lions are really good at?

Getting to the bottom-line
Organization
Task oriented projects
Bullet point conversations
Results
Making quick decisions
Being the leader

What do the other animals REALLY think about Lions?

Aggressive
Overbearing/Controlling
Too black and white
"My way or the highway"
Abrupt

**What ONE animal of the other
three animals "bugs" Lions the
most? Why?**

Most of the Lions across the
country pick the Lamb. Why? The
Lions and the Lambs are polar
opposites, s*ee the chart on page 69.*
The Lambs tend to be too passive;
they can't make quick decisions,
and the Lions never know when
the Lambs are going to get
emotional. Lions tend to not like
when people show their emotions.
Lions also say that Lambs don't
take a position. Remember the
Lions like the bottom-line, the
Lambs like a little conversation
which drives the Lions crazy!

**How do the other animals best
communicate with Lions for
the best results?**

Talk with bullet points. Give the
Lions the bottom-line. The Lions
have said loud and clear, don't

come to them with just the problem; come with solutions as well. Then THEY will make the final decision on the solution. If you are communicating with Lions, think of your voice and your words as staccato. Communicate with quick-to-the-point-words. No fluff.

Tidbits to Remember

If you work with a Lion,
"Get it Done."
They are task-oriented/leaders
A Lion's motivation is
FUNCTIONALITY.

Dark Side (My way or the highway)

Under pressure and stress, the Lions will get aggressive and shut people down. That is how you know something is wrong at work or home. They will use their hands more and sometimes get louder

than usual. Lions are usually
assertive, not aggressive.

How to Overcome

To lighten up the Lions' DARK
side, as much as possible, keep
them in the loop. This means at
home and at work. They like to be
in charge--*remember*? So let them
know if there might be a potential
crisis with a project at home or
work. If they receive a heads-up
before the crisis hits, they are more
likely not to turn dark.

Best Job

Lions are people who like goals,
respect, bottom-line and authority.
Lions like a job that means "I'm in
charge!"

CEO
Project Manager
Police Officer

14

Fireman/women
Doctors

Candy's Corner

How do Lions eat M&M's?
They wait for the Lambs to feed
the M&M's to them.

What is their favorite candy bar?
Hershey Bar: bottom-line, it's just
chocolate.

Whirling Around

(For adults only!)
Flirting Lions have a target, they
stay focused, and they are very
intentional with the end result in
mind.

"Staff and leaders who attended the retreat are raving about how they have been able to take the concepts and tools you taught during the Animal Game and are applying them in their every day work with clients, co-workers and community partners. Some have also been thrilled to be able to apply this new knowledge to their family members!"
--A. Webb, Social Work Supervisor

Chapter III

LAMB People

The Real Deal

Lambs are associated with obedience and due to widespread understanding and perceptions; they are not intelligent and have a herd mentality.
Wikipedia, 12/24/06.

Lamb Tango

When you see a Lamb dancing, you most likely see two dances--square dancing and the limbo. Square dancing is perfect for the Lambs because they love to be with a team, and they are great at following directions. Square dancing callers love the Lambs. Why the limbo? Simply, the Lambs will bend over backwards for anyone. They are the doers in an organization and at home.

What I Know

Many people believe because Lambs need a little more time to think or make a decision, they are not intelligent. Untrue! They simply want to take their time to make the right decision. Lambs are very team oriented and gentle. Lambs are usually the glue that holds the company together. They are the peacemakers that just want everyone to get along. I tease the Lambs and tell folks who work with them that you know who they are because they usually have a candy dish on their desks. Lambs in my audience always turn red and agree.

Animal Game Questions

From around the country, Lambs
responded to these questions.

What are things Lambs are really good at?

Open minded
Great team players
People oriented
Like conversation
Empathetic
Helping others
Peacemakers

What do the other animals REALLY think about Lambs?

Wishy-washy
Too passive
Indecisive
Pushover
Not competent

What ONE animal of the other three animals "bugs" the Lambs the most? Why?

The Lambs usually pick Lions because they say, "Lions can be mean!" The Lambs and the Lions are polar opposites, *see the chart on page 69.* They just don't like Lions' assertive, bottom-line tone. The Lambs comment that the Lions are just too aggressive and pushy. The Lambs feel the Lions need to give a little more detail, or have a conversation rather than just being short and to the point to get their message across.

How do the other animals best communicate with the Lambs for the best results?

The Lambs like face-to-face communication. They don't need to be told what to do and how to do it. They also like for you to have an open mind. If you simply visit with

the Lambs about what is needed
and how you can help, that is all it
takes. Think....very friendly, calm,
and conversational and you will
have the cooperation of Lambs
immediately.

Tidbits to Remember

If you work with a Lamb,
"Get Along."
They are people-oriented/doers
Their motivation is FUSION.

Dark Side (Passive Aggressive)

Here is an example I hear
frequently during the Animal
Game from the Lambs and other
animals. People ask Lambs for help
a lot. Why? Because they will
help. Remember: the Lambs are
people oriented and it is
in their DNA to be helpful. So
what happens? They help, help,

help until they cannot take it anymore. Then they find all the other Lambs they work with, and scream, complain and gossip and say, "I can't take it anymore, I do everything!" The Lambs usually become passive and aggressive when they are under pressure and stress. If you work or live with Lambs, you must recognize that when they are passive aggressive, something is wrong. This is not who they truly are, and they need to talk about how they are feeling.

How to Overcome

To lighten up the Lambs' dark side, first, let them talk! They really need to talk about what is on their plates. Then help them prioritize their many things on their to-do list. As leaders, you may offer the Lambs a "How to Say NO" class.

Best Job

Lambs are great listeners who are kind and helpful. For any job which means care giving, Lambs are perfect.

Teacher
Nurse
Receptionist
Administrative Assistant
Social Worker
Nanny

Candy's Corner

How do Lambs eat M&M's?
They eat them one at a time and they most certainly share them.

What is a Lamb's favorite candy bar? Three Musketeers: It's about a team!

Whirling Around

(For adults only!)
As flirts Lambs are subtle, almost
shy, quiet, charming and very
"other" focused.

Chapter IV

OWL People

The Real Deal

Owls are solitary. They are far-sighted and can't see much when objects are a few inches away, and they turn their heads 270°. Wikipedia, 12/24/06.

Owl Tango

The dance for the Owl is the Waltz. The Waltz is a very methodical dance. It's as simple as one-two-three, one-two-three. The dance is logical with no free style involved. It is a system.

What I Know

Owls need to see all the details. They are very analytical, research and data driven. If you are

25

working with Owls, you must be organized and prepared before you approach them. If you are married to an Owl, you better know your facts. You will always be asked who, what when, where and why by the Owls!

"I can't control what happens to me, but I can control how I react. You don't have to like people to cope with them; they are not difficult they are just different."

--Joe G., Business Owner
Workshop Participant

What are things the Owls are really good at?

Analysis
Details
Task oriented
Like lists
Thorough
Accurate

What do the other animals REALLY think about Owls?

Anal Retentive
Perfectionist
Too detail oriented
Rigid
Passive
Too rule driven

What ONE animal of the other three animals "bugs" Owls the most? Why?

The Owls almost always choose the
Chameleons. The Owls and
Chameleons are polar opposites,
see the chart on page 69. The Owls
believe that the Chameleons are
too impulsive, they make decisions
too fast or they flip-flop on the
decision they just made. The Owls
also comment that the Chameleons
don't do enough research to get the
right answers.

How do the other animals best communicate with Owls for the best results?

Owls like detail. When you approach them have the research and data on hand. The Owls across the country want email first.....it's documentation. Make sure the email is more detailed then say a Lions bullet pointed email. Give the Owls lists, charts and graphs; it will be a happy day! This may take a little more time, but you will have more cooperative Owls with more detail. You can never have too much detail for this group.

Tidbits to Remember

If you work with an Owl,
"Get it Right."
They are task-oriented/doers
Owls' motivation is FACTS.

28

Dark Side (Leave me alone)

If Owls do not receive all the facts
and details they need, they cannot
move on with either a personal or a
professional project. Without the
information they need to make the
right decisions about the project,
they will just shut down and say,
"Leave me alone!"

How to Overcome

To lighten up the Owls' dark side,
get the information the Owls need,
and they will be happy, as will you.
One Owl that I know well, said, "If
you are working for or with an Owl
get them to do the research and
pull the facts together. It is the
best way for them to contribute,
and they enjoy it."

Best Job

These are people who are exacting, focused, precise and detail oriented.

Accountant
Engineer
IT Specialist
Scientist
Architect
Technical Writer
Analyst

Candy's Corner

How do Owls eat M&M's?
They lay them all out, separate them by color and eat one color at a time.

What is the Owl's favorite candy bar? Kit Kat: It can be split into four precise, perfect pieces.

[Note: As I was writing this piece my husband the Owl said, "Don't you need to do research to see if this is truly the Owl's favorite candy bar?" He's such an Owl.] My informal research resulted from asking folks across the country during my speaking engagements.

Whirling Around

(For adults only!)
To flirt, Owls first send an email or voicemail with hopes that the person is not there, so they can leave a very detailed message with steps to take for the other to respond.

"I just wanted to drop you a line and tell you about the marked improvement in our workplace relationships since you delivered your motivating message and the Animal Game to our staff. The historically divided lines between administrative and legal peer groups, has all but disappeared. The office goals are now achieved in an environment of unified collaboration. Thanks for your insightful, inspiring, and conscious raising exercises. You are a credit to your profession and a quality catalyst to others."

--D. de Clue, CSE Lead Supervisor,

Chapter V

The LB's and NT's Technique:
Talk to the Animals

It's hard in our busy world to pay attention to our communication skills, yet it's a must if we want to be effective communicators.

Verbal communication is more than knowing what the words mean. It's the art of choosing your words wisely for any situation. I've learned that one of the most difficult situations people encounter is giving constructive feedback in a straightforward yet positive way. Although difficult, constructive, straightforward feedback is essential if positive relationships are to be maintained. I teach a method that I call the Like Best and Next Time technique, LB's and NT's for short.

This is language I learned when I attended a certification program at Fred Pryor Seminars on how to become a better presenter. With practice using this language, you will enhance your verbal communication skills and your working relationships. Let me give you an example of how the Like Best and Next Time technique was used with me at the workshop I attended.

I had to do a 15-minute presentation on Leadership Skills. I did this presentation in front of my supervisors and peers. While I was doing the presentation, the group was evaluating me by observing and taking notes. When I was finished, they gave me constructive feedback by using the Like-Best and Next-Time language.

The group's feedback was
summarized by one evaluator:
> "Candy, I really **liked** your
> humor in the introduction
> and how you interacted with
> the audience. **Next time** I
> would slow down a little.
> The presentation was
> supposed to be 15 minutes
> and it was 12 minutes.
> Before you sit down Candy, I
> want to add that I really
> **liked** your activity, it was
> relevant to the lesson you
> were teaching the group."

The Like-Best and Next-Time language is this simple. It's up to you to be proactive and think ahead of time about what you're going to say to your recipient. Consider some key points before you try this new language:

- Always start with what you like best about the person, some positives. This approach builds confidence and receptivity to the constructive feedback.

- If you go back to the example, you will notice the words "but" or "however" were not used before they gave me my constructive feedback (next times). What happens when someone gives you a positive or "like best," then gives you a "but" or "however?" You guessed it. It negates all of the positive things they just said. Participants in my workshops have asked me

why they shouldn't use
"however," and I tell them
that "however" is a "but" in a
tuxedo! So be careful.

NTK's (Need to Knows)

When you talk to the animals, be clear about the LB's and NT's.

Scenario: You have someone you work with who did not get their piece of a project finished by the deadline and you need to speak to them about this….give them some LB's and NT's.

Scripts

Chameleon (LB's & NT's)

Give the Chameleon's two LB's up front. Remember, they like appreciation. Give them the feedback and give them options because they like choices. End with more appreciation.

Example:

LB— Hey, I just want to let you know how much I appreciate the work you have done so far on the project. Also, great job on working with our vendors.
NT—I noticed the deadline was missed on October 15th for the last piece, and it's slowing the rest of the project down. When is the soonest you can get your piece to me, this morning or afternoon? Do you need more resources?
LB—Thanks for getting your piece to me. We couldn't do this without you.

Lion (LB's & NT's)

Keep in mind, Lions like the "bottom-line," so be short and to the point. It would be helpful to think in bullet points.

Example:

LB—Not sure what happened with the deadline. This is unusual for you. You are usually so organized.
NT—We need your piece of the project by Oct. 16th. Will that work?
LB—Thanks.

Note: Lambs, I know this script sounds abrupt and aggressive. The Lions across the country whom I work with say, "It's not abrupt!" They beg the Lambs to talk like this.

Lamb (LB's & NT's)

Use the Lamb's language when giving the LB's and NT's. For example, use words such as team, we, all of us. Also, remember the small talk when talking to the Lambs.

Example:

LB—How are you today? How was your weekend? Great job on the last project your team worked on last quarter.

NT-- I noticed that your piece of our recent project was not finished by the deadline and this may affect the rest of the team. I would like to know if anything is going on, this is unusual for you? Do you need help finishing up by Oct. 16th?

LB—Thanks for all you do. The team really appreciates your work and dedication.

41

Note: Lions, I can hear you. "Blah, blah, blah--I don't have time to be nicey, nicey." If you would be a little nicey, you will get better work from the Lambs. Take the time and trust me!

Owl (LB's & NT's)

Owls like precise language. More than the Lion's bullet points, they want an extended list with more detail.

Example:

LB—Your efficiency was appreciated on the last project. **NT**—That is why I was so surprised when you missed the Oct. 15th deadline as shown here on the timeline I provided. *[Have two copies of the timeline, one for you and one for the Owl.]* **LB**—Thank you for all the research you have done so far. We appreciate your efficiency. Let me know if you need my help. *[Note: they won't.]*

Remember:
All the animals appreciate the LB's and NT's, and each script is expressed a little differently and

43

it's those differences that will make all the difference in your communication.

Chapter VI

Stories from You!

Story I

When my daughter Alex was 13 years old, I taught her the concepts of the Animal Game. She had seen me present the game at one of my workshops and was curious about it. After I explained the personality styles of the animals to her, she started analyzing her friends and teachers.

A few years later, her knowledge came in handy. Alex had been in her high school biology class the first semester and was doing well and loved her teacher. Next semester she came back after spring break and she had been transferred to another class with another teacher. She came home after the third day with the new

45

teacher and said, "Mom, you have to help me. I was transferred into another biology class. They said my first class was overcrowded, and this new teacher is an OWL!"

Alex proceeded to explain to me that her first semester teacher was a Chameleon, and she taught with examples, she was interactive and made the class fun. The second semester teacher used PowerPoint, read from the book, and lectured.

Alex said, "Mom, you know I don't learn that way. I am a Chameleon, so I need interaction or I just get tired in class and I want to sleep! What should I do?" [*First, let me say that this was a mother's dream, my teenage daughter actually listened and learned something I taught her. I heard harps, and the angels swirled around my head!*]

After my feet touched the ground again, I told Alex to go to her

counselor and use the same
language she used with me to
explain her issue, in a calmer tone
of voice. It worked! She was
moved back into her original class,
did very well and was a much
happier student.

Lesson: teach the animal
personality styles to your children.
By ages 11 to 13 they are ready.
Children are smart, so don't sell
them short. The Animal Game will
help them with friends, siblings,
parents, bosses and teachers!

What Kids Need to Know

<u>Chameleon</u>

Your Teachers-
- Interactive, use activities to teach the lessons, have humor, let you work in groups.

Your Parents-
- Little more laid back, fun, open minded, give you choices, but change their mind.

Your Friends-
- Fun, like to joke around, not real focused, like choices, change their mind…a lot.

Lion

Your Teachers-
- Likes for you to be short and to the point when you ask a question, work with bullet points, expect a lot from you.

Your Parents-
- Like for you to listen to them, short conversations, like to have fun but the fun needs to be organized.

Your Friends-
- Don't smile as much as others, pretty serious thinker, like to be in charge of the plans, usually is the leader.

Lamb

Your Teachers-
- Will be nice and soft spoken, they will listen to your side; they will let you work in groups.

Your Parents-
- Kind, open minded, give you choices, they don't like to argue so you might get your way more...but not a good lesson because you won't always get your way in the future.

Your Friends-
- Nice, kind of shy, they like for others to make the decision on what to do, everyone likes them.

<u>Owl</u>

Your Teachers-
- Like to use graphs, charts and PowerPoint. They don't use many activities, and when asked questions they will ask one back....so be ready.

Your Parents-
- They like the details of who you are with, where are you going and EXACTLY when you will be home. They like rules.

Your Friends-
- They like details, they are not going to randomly pick what to do, and they will have to do a little research before they do something. They tend to be quiet. They will talk when they believe it is necessary.

Story II

After I spoke at a social and rehabilitation facility, my client sent this great story about one of her staff members.

"The communication activity you did with the staff has left a lasting impression. One staff member related a story to me about how your presentation improved her ability to communicate with other "animals." She had been frustrated by a co-worker who never responded to her emails during the years they had worked together. After hearing your presentation on the different communication styles, she identified this co-worker's "animal" and decided to write the email as if she were the same "animal." Guess what happened next? The co-worker emailed her back for the first time! Your presentation gave our staff real techniques that they have actually applied to their daily work."

Story III

One Friday after I spoke at a local
Chamber of Commerce meeting,
two of my participants, Marcus and
John, were interested in my other
workshops and wanted to hire me
to work with their respective
companies' leadership teams.
*[Reader, here is your first pop quiz!
See if you can identify which
animal my clients could be.]*
After the meeting, Marcus came up
to me and said, "You were being
auditioned today. I'll be in touch."

Marcus calls: "Candy, you did a
great job. I want to hire you. Is
November 24th open on your
calendar? Good. How much do you
charge? I'll get back to you."

 (The following Monday morning)
"Candy we're on for November 24th.
Park across the street. We'll see
you on the 24th."

Who is Marcus? GRRRRR! You guessed it, a Lion. How did I respond knowing he is a Lion? Yes. No. OK!

John emails: "Candy, my name is John and I am the training coordinator for my company. I was at the Chamber of Commerce meeting one month ago, which was great. I don't expect you to remember me with all the workshops you do, but the person you were talking to before you presented was one of my bosses. We would like to visit with you about working with our leadership group about Human Relations and Communication Skills and thought you would be perfect for our needs. Viewing your website and topics and watching your video demos gave me the boost again today like I had when I left the Chamber meeting. How can we further discuss bringing you in to see if you can help us with your expertise?"

Who is John? BAAAAA! You're right a Lamb. John was adorable and I did remember him because he had a very kind conversation with me after the meeting.

I hope you can see the differences and hear them too. I knew Marcus needed no conversation from me, he just needed the bottom-line, date, time, fee. John on the other hand needed more. I called John right after I received his email and had a conversation about what was going on in the company, including the good things, the bad things, and the personalities of the leadership team.

Both clients have proven to be great clients and easy to work with....why? Because I learned very quickly about how to work with each of them.

Story IV

I was recently visiting with one of
my clients about the Animal Game.
I had taught the activity at a
previous workshop for this client,
so she was familiar with the
personality style differences. My
client told me about a recent lesson
she learned about the Lions. She
recently had a birthday, and she
received an unusual gift. This
particular company has a
"Celebration Committee" who are
employees who have volunteered to
make homemade gifts or baked
goods to celebrate different
holidays for the managers and
employees. The volunteers will
make cookies, cupcakes or a cake
for birthdays and anniversaries.
For my client's birthday, a member
of the celebration committee
dashed into my client's office and
all but threw her birthday cookie
on her desk. The cookie was in
four pieces! The volunteer said,

"That must have happened in the car." My client said when she looked at the cookie she could tell that it was baked that way--in pieces. She also noted how disgruntled the volunteer was, as if she had been forced to participate. My client always knew this volunteer was a LION and she had no idea why she was on this committee!

I laughed until I cried when my client told me this story! Lions should stick to organizing, not making gifts. Leave that part to the Chameleons and Lambs.

Chapter VII

What I Hear from You!

I use my Animal Game as a tool when I am presenting stress management, leadership skills, team building, and creativity. So I teach it a lot. Some of the comments I hear are funny, sometimes nasty, but most of all real! When you read these comments, please keep in mind they are perspectives from the animals. Also, keep in mind that the comment could have come from you!

Comments from the Animal Game:

When asked what the perceived negatives of the animal were, the spokesperson for the Chameleons turned to the other Chameleons and asked, *"What did we say, no*

*that's not it, didn't we say
this…OH…. I can't remember! Oh,
yes….we're wishy-washy!"*
I love when the truth comes out!

The Lions were asked the same
question. The spokes-Lion said, as
he was hitting his hand with his
fist, *"People think we are aggressive
and pushy!!!"*
Almost every time the Lions say
this, the Lambs very subtly and
quietly nod, just enough so I can
see, but the Lions never catch it.

The Owls are funny birds. They
don't say much during the Animal
Game, but what I do see is many of
them are feverously taking notes
the entire time. This is usually no
big deal, but I always tell my
groups to just get into the activity,
don't take notes. The Owls just
look at me with their "Whatever"
looks as they grab their pens and
paper. I am laughing as I write
this because I have been married to

an Owl for many years!

The Things I Know

Myers-Briggs is a complicated personality instrument that, for the sake of simplicity, I am avoiding here. The other instruments are more readily matched to the Animal Game. You will find the matches to DISC, SELF, or True Colors personality indicators, below:

Chameleons, you are the....
 "I" in **DISC**
"S" in **SELF**
"Orange" in **True Colors**

Lions, you are the...
 "D" in **DISC**
"E" in **SELF**
"Gold" in **True Colors**

Lambs, you are the…
 "S" in **DISC**
"L" in **SELF**
"Blue" in **True Colors**

Owls, you are the…
 "C" in **DISC**
"F" in **SELF**
"Green" in **True Colors**

Chapter VIII

Animal Game

This game provides participant players with great opportunities for learning and appreciating different personality styles of family and team members. Therefore, the game is great for communication, negotiation, teambuilding, problem solving.

Supplies Needed

8 ½" X 11" colored sheets with one each of these animals' names: **Chameleon, Lion, Lamb, Owl.** Draw the Animal Game Chart from page 69 on a flipchart or drawing board for use after question #3 is answered during the game.

How to Play:

Start by describing some of the characteristics of each animal from the previous chapters. I usually give my group three or four characteristics of each animal then I tell them to go stand by the animal sign that best describes them after hearing those characteristics. If during the Animal Game people start feeling like they are truly another animal; I tell them they can *defect* to the right animal.

Have them answer the following four questions. If the group is more than 10 people per animal, then divide them into smaller groups.

Questions:

1. What are two things your animal is really good at, what are your strengths?

2. What do the other animals think about you? What are their perceptions?

3. Choosing from the three other animals in the room, which one animal "bugs" your animal the most and why? (Refer to Animal Game Chart on page 69)

4. How do the other animals' communicate with your animal for best results?

What differs with the answers given during the Animal Game depends on the demographics of the groups. For example, if I have a group with all leaders, the answers may differ from a group from a manufacturing plant. The answers are also the animals' perceptions.

At the end of the Animal Game give the participants a pop quiz to see if they truly understand the differences.

Pop Quiz Example

Give the animals a scenario: "You are having an issue (pick any issue) with a peer at work and you need to talk to them about it... Chameleon, your peer is an Owl. Lion, your peer is a Lamb. Owl, your peer is a Chameleon. Lamb, your peer is a Lion. Ask them how they would approach and communicate with someone who is not like them. Give the groups about two minutes to discuss with their fellow animals, and then have them face the animal that they have been assigned and give their answer. The animals that are receiving can give a thumbs-up if they agree with the communication or a thumbs-down if they disagree. If they disagree, ask them to give an explanation of what they disagreed about.

[Note: Sometimes during my Animal Game, the Lambs will say

66

the Lions were too patronizing in their conversation. The Lions will say the Lambs talked too much. I actually like it when this happens because we may think we are doing a good job communicating with a different animal, yet often we are way off track! This takes practice and patience, but it works.]

* Do this if you have time: have the attendees go back to their seats, and have them, as a group, write down three conclusions or observations they had while playing the Animal Game.

WARNING

If you get frustrated or confused in teaching the Animal Game, contact me. Doing something new can feel as if you are on a roller coaster that's out of control. Just stay buckled up and I'll help, so the adventure can continue!

Candy Whirley's contact info:
Email cwhirley@kc.rr.com
Websites www.candywhirley.com
          www.nsaspeaker.org
          www.nsa-heartland.org
          www.linkedin.com
          www.facebook.com

Animal Game Chart

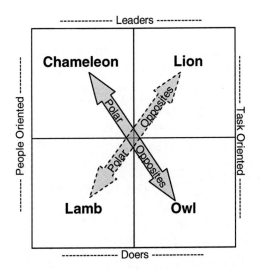

CONCLUSION

I hope you enjoyed the book as much as I did writing it! This way of teaching personality differences has proven to be the best lesson I teach across the country. People truly get it, and I learn with them!

You must keep this book in your purse, pocket or briefcase. Put a copy in your desk drawer at work and at home. You will need multiple copies, and I promise you, your life and tango will be easier if you know who you are communicating, negotiating and dancing with at all times!

So go out there and start dancing....not *your* tango, but **their** tango! The results will be a tango you have never danced! Remember: It Takes 4 to TANGO!

Cue tango music........................

RESOURCES

Cooke, R., & Marston, W. (2000). *The ama disc survey*. 1st ed. New York: Center for Applied Research.

Goby, V., & Lewis, J. (2000). Using experiential learning theory and the Myers Briggs type indicator in teaching business communication. *Business Communication Quarterly, 63* (3), 39-48.

Miscisin, M. True Color Personality Test. Retrieved Feb. 09. http://www.truecolorstest.com/True _Colors_Test.sh ml

SELF Profile. National Press Publications, Div. of Rockhurst Univ. Continuous Education Ctr.

What is the True Color Personality Test? Retrieved Feb. 09. http://www.truecolorspersonalityte st.com/what-is-true-colors-personality.htm

To Share "It Takes 4 To Tango"

Books—To order a copy of this book for a friend, colleague, associate, or loved one, check online:
www.candywhirley.com

For multiple-copy discounts, please call 816-304-9933.

Keynote Speech and/or Training—To have Candy speak at your next event, call the above number. You'll find details at the above website.

"Candy, you make understanding the differences between people important, enlightening, and entertaining as well. I can tell you that getting Wal-Mart managers to sit and go through a training topic can be tough at times as they are very accustomed to the go, go, go mentality, yet your facilitation made it very interactive and allowed the managers to have fun".
K. Dailey, General Manager, Wal-Mart

It Takes 4 to Tango 30-Day Avanoo Program Journal

YES! You can get more Candy and put her in your pocket for
30 days!
Want to be a part of Candy's 30-Day Avanoo Program? go to her website
www.candywhirley.com
or email
candy@candywhirley.com

Day One

It Takes 4 To Tango...If you work and live with PEOPLE!

Today I want you to think about what personality or Animal you think you are so far...now...you will want to pick more than 1, but pick the one you feel strongest about and then your goal is to write down 2-3 things you are really good at, what are your best qualities?

Day Two

Get to know the Chameleon

Think about the people in your personal
and professional life who you think are
Chameleons. Write down their names
(don't post this on social media yet) now
beside each name I want you to add their
strengths and their positive influences in
your life or on your team?

Day Three

A few things to look out for, with a Chameleon

If you are a Chameleon think about those times of stress…and how that felt….and what you said. Now, forgive your actions and come up with a quick breathing exercise for next time that happens. Write down what you will commit to doing next time this happens, what are some things you can do that will help curve that sharp tongue or help a Chameleon de-stress?

Day Four

True strengths of the Chameleon...what are they good at?

Today...I want you to write down the names of those Chameleons you work with. Now beside each name I want you to write down one way you can give them a little recognition.

Day Five

Chameleons...under stress!

Today, take a moment to write down one thing you will proactively do next time you are in a situation where your Chameleon co-worker or manger shows one of their weaknesses.

Day Six

Who is the Chameleon's polar opposite?

Today, take some time to think about the
Owl in your life. Instead of thinking about
how they drive you crazy write down 2-3
positive things they bring to the table that
makes your life easier. If you ARE the
Owl, then it's time to celebrate what you
bring to folks in your life who are your
polar opposites, resolve today to continue
to complement their strengths however
you can!

Day Seven

More thoughts and lessons about the Chameleon

Today I want you to do two things: First, think about one thing you can do to motivate that Chameleon you work with. Second, write down a sentence you will use as a "self-dialogue" next time you have a misperception about a Chameleon, for example when you are thinking "This Chameleon is a scatter brain!" Your self-dialogue might be: "I realize the Chameleons can tend to be high energy and have several different ways of doing things, I need to be open to their ideas."

Day Eight

Final Chameleon story

Think about who you could share this knowledge with. Today, write down 2-3 lessons you have learned about the Chameleon. I also want you to write down how you will use those lessons to your benefit.

Day Nine

Get to Know the Lion

Think about the Lions you work with or maybe live with. Write the names of at least 3 Lions in your life. Beside their names write down one thing you will do differently next time you take their actions personally.

Day Ten

A few things to look out for with a Lion

Think about the one or two Lions in your life right now and write their names down. Next to those names write how you will approach them next time you need to communicate with them.

Day Eleven

True strengths of the Lion...what are they good at?

Take a minute today, and think about all the Lions in your life...the ones you like and the ones you don't like. Now write down at least one strength of the Lion's in your life and how that strength can help you in your personal or professional life.

Day Twelve

Lions...under stress!

Think about a time you were in the presence of a stressed out Lion, feel those feelings. Now right down what you will do next time this happens.. now that you know what you know about the stressed Lion. Remember: Don't take it personally☺

Day Thirteen

Who is the Lion's polar opposite?

If you are a Lion write down the name of your polar opposite Lamb (probably your significant other.) Now write down one thing you will do next time that Lamb drives you crazy. What can you do to enhance the relationship instead of hindering it?

Day Fourteen

More thoughts and lessons about the Lion

Picture that Lion right now...visualize them upset...now visualize what you could do to help them solve a problem...will you talk it out? No. Write down what you would do. Remember not to expect praise and let it GO.

Day Fifteen

Get to know the Lamb

Today think about the Lambs in your life. What are two things you want to do differently while working with Lambs? If you are a Lamb, pick one person in your life you want to tell. Share your characteristics so they will understand you differently...or maybe even better.

Day Sixteen

A few things to look out for with a Lamb

Think about the Lambs in your professional or personal life. Write down the names of the Lambs who are closest to you. Now write down one or two interactive strategies that will make your relations with these people more effective.

Day Seventeen

True strengths of the Lamb...what are they good at?

Think about the Lambs you work with. Now write their names down and beside each name write down the best working situation in which these particular Lambs would most likely be successful.

Day Eighteen

Lambs...under stress!

If you are a Lamb write down three things you want to change so you don't get taken advantage of or have too much on your plate. If you work or live with a Lamb write down 3 things you will do next time you work to them.

Day Nineteen

Who is the Lamb's polar opposite?

Think about your Lion polar opposites and write their names down. Beside their names write down one thing you will do differently next time you have to communicate or work them. This could be things you could do differently in an email or in person.

Day Twenty

More thoughts and lessons about the Lamb

If you are a Lamb think about one or two things you can do to help the other animals understand YOU better. If you work with a Lamb what are one or two things you can ask your Lamb colleague to help you understand THEM better?

Day Twenty One

Get to Know the Owl

Today, simply think about the Owls in your life…picture them. Maybe you are the Owl? What are one or two things you can do to better work with Owls in your work environment? If YOU are the Owl what are one or two things you can do to help the other animals understand you better?

Day Twenty Two

A few things to look for with an Owl

Today I want you to think about the one
Owl in your personal life and the one Owl
in your professional life. Write their
names down. Beside their names right
down one thing that drives you crazy.
Why? Now write down one thing you can
do to make that Owl's life easier.

Day Twenty Three

True strengths of the Owl...what are they good at?

Think about all the strengths of your Owl co-workers or Owl friends. What is one thing you could hand off to an Owl because of their great analytical strength? This may be something you just don't have time to do the research or YOU just don't want to do the research....it would be the Owl's pleasure☺

Day Twenty Four

Owls...under stress!

Think about the last time you were
working with an Owl and they shut down.
What is one thing you would differently,
now that you know that Owl might have
simply been stressed out?

Day Twenty Five

Who is the Owl's polar opposite?

If you are an Owl think about your polar opposite Chameleon. What could you do differently, Owl, to make this relationship easier? If you are a Chameleon think about your polar opposite Owl. What could you do differently, Chameleon, to make this relationship easier?

Day Twenty Six

More thoughts and lessons about the Owl

Think about all the Owls in your life. Write down 2 things you will do to help make the Owls in life easier at work or home.

Day Twenty Seven

Chameleon during change

Think about the last time you had to go through a major change at home or work. How did you react? If you are a Chameleon think about one way you could help others. If you are not a Chameleon think about what you could do to help them stay on track with the change.

Day Twenty Eight

Lion during change

If you are a Lion think about one way you could help others during change. If you are not a Lion...think about what you could do... to NOT get frustrated with their aggressiveness.

Day Twenty Nine

Lamb during change

If you are a Lamb think about one way
you could help others during change. If
you are not a Lamb...what could you do to
help the Lamb not get too wrapped up on
the personal side of the change?

Day Thirty

Owl during change and Wrap-Up

If you are an Owl think about one way you could help others during change. If you are not an Owl...what could you do to NOT get frustrated with their details they have to have?